An Early New England Seaport

ATLANTIC HOUSE

CUSTOM HOUSE

STARBUCK COOPER SHOP

CHINA TEA STORE

1745

STEAM BOAT EXCURSION

J. POTTLE, SHIPS CHANDLER

10 Cut and Assemble Buildings in H-O Scale
by Edmund V. Gillon Jr.

Edmund V. Gillon Jr. is a native New Englander, born in East Brimfield, Massachusetts in 1929. His lifelong interest in antiques and rural architecture was sparked while working as a guide at nearby Old Sturbridge Village. During his teenage years he made innumerable forays into the New England countryside, photographing the regional architecture, and making rubbings of ancient gravestones. The rubbing collection ultimately led to his book, *Early New England Gravestone Rubbings*, the first book to be published on that subject.

Mr. Gillon attended art school in Boston. After graduation he moved to New York City, where he worked in the art department of an advertising agency and later as a package designer for a cosmetic company. The engineering principles of folding box construction learned in package design, prompted Mr. Gillon to apply these principles to the cut and assemble architectural models which he began producing in book form. Thus, a new kind of book was born. His early publications include, *A New England Village*, *A Western Frontier Town*, *Victorian Houses*, and *A Pennsylvania Dutch Farm*. Later, with the inovation of movable parts, his paper craft books, included an up and down sawmill, a windmill, a catapult, and a guillotine.

Mr. Gillon has photographed New York City extensively during the thirty years he has lived there. His architectural photographs have been the subjects of several books relating to the New York scene such as *South Street Seaport*, *New York Civic Sculpture*, *The Great Sights of New York*, *New York Then and Now*, *Cast-iron Architecture in New York*, and *The Lower East Side*.

Creating his own outpost of New England in Manhattan, Mr. Gillon lives in an 1850's Brownstone garden apartment, in the shadow of the Empire State Building, decorated with numerous primitive antiques.

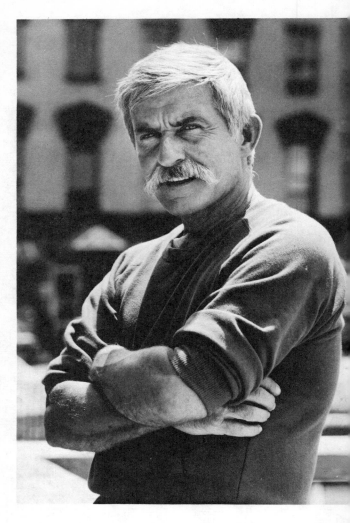

Printed in the United States of America.
ISBN: 0-88740-063-9
Published by Schiffer Publishing Ltd.
1469 Morstein Road
West Chester, Pennsylvania 19380

This book may be purchased from the publisher.
Please include $1.50 postage.
Try your bookstore first.

Introduction

The early settlers of the New England coast were not practiced seamen. Most were farmers or artisans supporting the agricultural life, delivered to the new world by mariners who then sailed back to England. A short growing season and a rock strewn landscape were two of the factors that resulted in a disenchantment among the colonists who attempted to eke out a living in farming. They were soon attracted to the more abundant harvests of the sea. House carpenters and smiths turned their talents to the building of structures that would float, giving birth to the famous New England shipbuilding industry of the eighteenth and nineteenth century.

The New England coast with its innumerable inlets provided well protected harbors and great ports sprang up such as Boston, Salem, Portsmouth, Newburyport, New Bedford, Providence and New London. Whaling, fishing, shipbuilding and trade were the basis of these ports' economy. Great fortunes were ammassed and the seaports became the region's most cosmopolitan communities. The China trade in the nineteenth century resulted in the import of exotic treasures from around the world.

The buildings contained within this book represent some of the types of structures that might have been found in the waterfront districts of a typical small New England seaport in the latter part of the eighteenth and the early 19th century. Each building is a replica of an actual structure. The following ports are where these structures are located: Nantucket, Massachusetts (Captain's House, Mariners Church, Greek Revival Cottage and Cooper Shop); Marblehead, Massachusetts (Atlantic House Inn, Custom House); Rockport, Massachusetts (Gambrel Roofed Cottage); Ipswich, Massachusetts (Blue Anchor Tavern); Portsmouth, New Hampshire (Warehouse and Ships Chandler).

Captains House

The above view is of the former whaling port of Nantucket, Massachusetts, an island located 30 miles off the New England coast. In its hey-dey, in the 1840's Nantucket had close to ten thousand inhabitants, a fleet of ninety whaling vessels, and the distinction of being the greatest whaling port in the world. Its great prosperity was not reflected in its architecture, which tended to be of an austere nature. This was accounted for by the spartan taste of the Quaker builders.

A regional style of domestic architecture developed. The following description of a typical Nantucket house is an illustration: The house consists of two stories with attic; the basement is high with walls of brick, pierced by windows of considerable size; the front door is off-center; the massive brick chimney is located to one side of center; the roof is gable without dormers. Surmounting the ridge pole of the roof is a "walk"—a most distinctive Nantucket feature, that consists of a platform surrounded by a railing. The principal motivation for the roof walk seems to have been a fear of fire! The busy seaman's wife was more likely to have used it for dumping a bucketful of sand or water down the burning chimney, than idly searching for a sail, as we have been led to believe.

Instructions

The following basic tools are recommended: an x-acto knife & #11 blade; a scoring tool to create folds; a burnishing tool for pressing down glue tabs in areas difficult to reach with fingertips; a clear plastic triangle to use as a cutting and scoring guide; Elmers glue. Dots indicate glue tabs, x's indicate areas to be cut out. Apply glue to tabs only, not to the receiving surface. Do not apply too much glue—it will seep out and mar the printed surface. The vertical lines of fence should be cut before removing fence from background sheet. Next, glue upper & lower horizontal braces to areas indicated on fence, then cut out fence area. Insert brace tips into slits in fence posts (pieces 14, 16 and 19). Glue piece 18 to inside midway point of fence section (piece 13).

Circles indicate eaves. To create the overhang, cut underneath base of gable triangle to corner fold line.

To secure seagulls to roof, cut small slit in roof ridge and insert gull leg. Add black dot for eye and color beak yellow on opposite side of printed surface.

Captains House

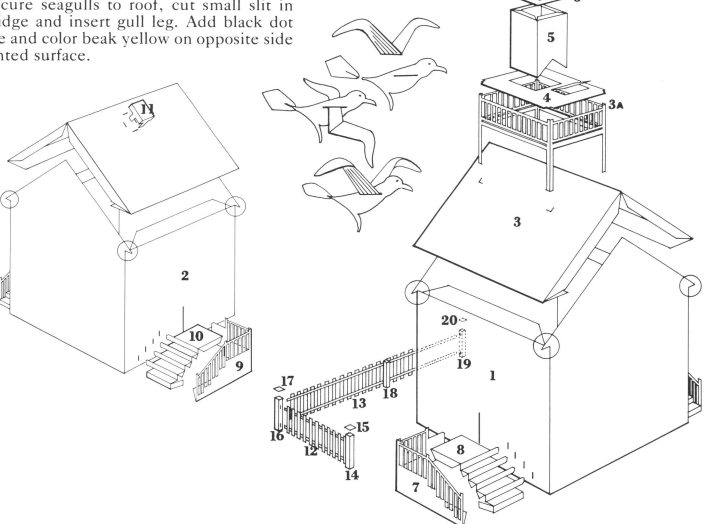

Greek Revival Cottage

The architectural style known as Greek Revival took hold in America around the year 1820. Greek architecture symbolized the earliest democracy in the world. The style was warmly received in America where there was a strong sympathy for the Greek War for independence from Turkey in 1821.

This sympathy resulted in making all things Greek a national fashion. The temple shape was ideally suited to the traditional gable-roofed house. By turning the gable end to the street, and applying a portico, a modest dwelling gained an impressive dignity. Even without the portico, corner pilasters, a frieze beneath the eaves or a Greek style enframement at the doorway, served the same purpose. An existing house simply painted white became a reasonable facsimile of Greek marble. It was a popular style within the reach of the masses, and it gained a startling proliferation throughout the nation.

Greek Revival Cottage

The vertical lines of fence should be cut before removing fence from background sheet. Next, glue upper & lower horizontal braces to areas indicated on fence, then cut out fence area. Insert brace tips into slits in fence posts (pieces 8 & 11).

Circles indicate eaves. To create the overhang, cut underneath base of gable triangle to corner fold line.

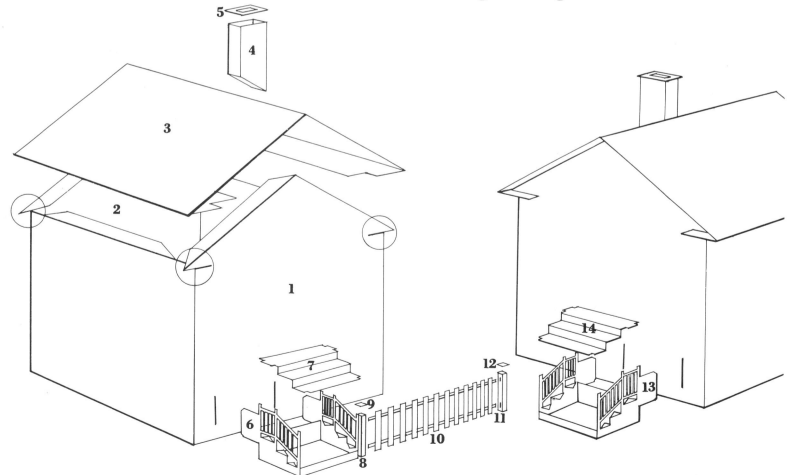

Lamb Tavern, Washington St., Boston, Mass.

Early New England Taverns

The waterfront taverns with their swinging heraldic signs, bearing such names as "The Bunch of Grapes," "The Harp and Crown" or "Ship Aground" were a welcome sight to seamen and merchants in such places of great commerce as Salem, Newburyport, Portsmouth, Newport, Boston and New Bedford. Warmth and comfort enveloped the patrons. The bar provided them with Medford and Jamaica Rum, Cider, Madeira, or hot spiced drinks. After 1830 cocktails and juleps were added to the fare, and toasts—so named because the hot toast floated in wine or spirits to warm a drink—had been in fashion since the Seventeenth Century.

Toasts were encouraged in the taverns, where the congenial atmosphere was conducive to relaxation and games of backgammon, dice, cards, or ninepins.

These early taverns were popular with the great as well as with the raffish. Romantic lore and touches of history often clung to these places.

Blue Anchor Tavern

Circles indicate eaves. To create the over-hang, cut underneath base of gable triangle to corner fold line.

To hang tavern sign (piece 12) insert tips of support arms thru slits in gable (piece 2).

Doors may be opened by cutting top, right and bottom edges, then score left edge and bend in or out as desired.

To secure seagulls to roof, cut small slit in roof ridge and insert gull leg. Add black dot for eye and color beak yellow on opposite side of printed surface.

New England Church

The early New England meeting house is symbolic of practically all that is characteristic of the New England way of life and thought. It was the nucleus of the early communities, the seat of local government, and the birthplace of that peculiarly New England institution—the town meeting. The meeting house or church possessed none of the sacredness in the minds of their builders, in contrast to the consecrated edifices in which their forefathers had worshipped in Old England. These New England buildings were used for all public town purposes. The drum, more often than the bell, was used to call the citizenry together, whether for worship or secular purposes. The white clapboard church with its clear glass windows, often framed by black or green shutters and its spire topped by a weathervane, dominated the skyline of most coastal ports and served as a landmark for returning ships.

Mariners Church

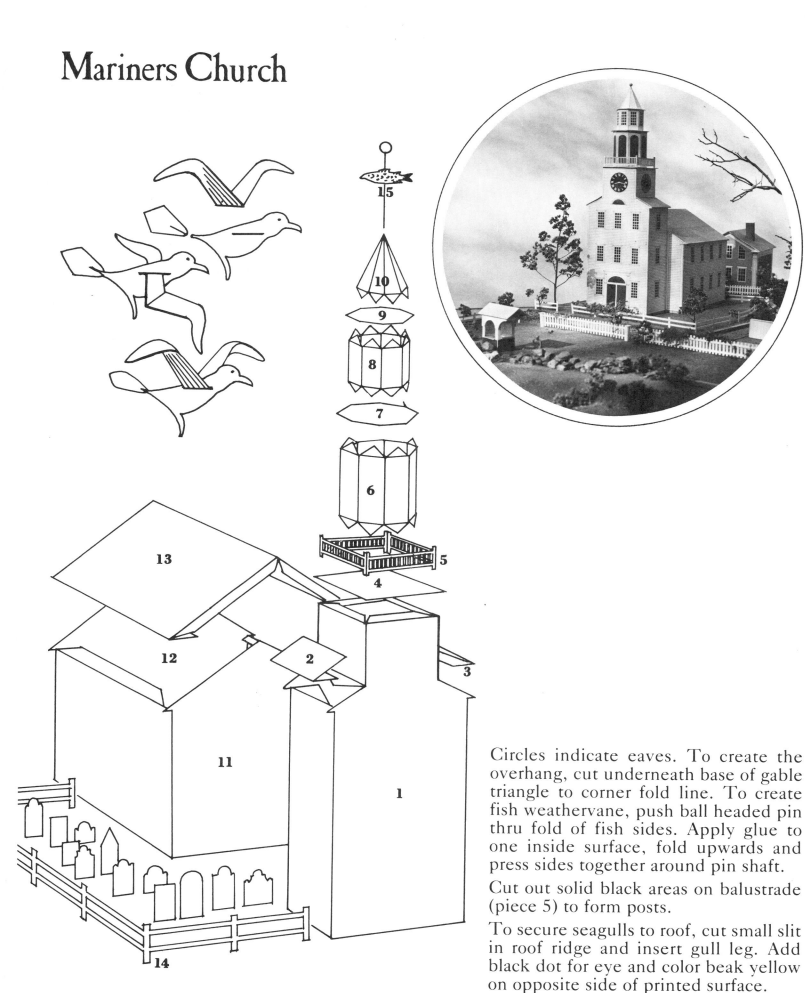

Circles indicate eaves. To create the overhang, cut underneath base of gable triangle to corner fold line. To create fish weathervane, push ball headed pin thru fold of fish sides. Apply glue to one inside surface, fold upwards and press sides together around pin shaft.

Cut out solid black areas on balustrade (piece 5) to form posts.

To secure seagulls to roof, cut small slit in roof ridge and insert gull leg. Add black dot for eye and color beak yellow on opposite side of printed surface.

Lighthouse

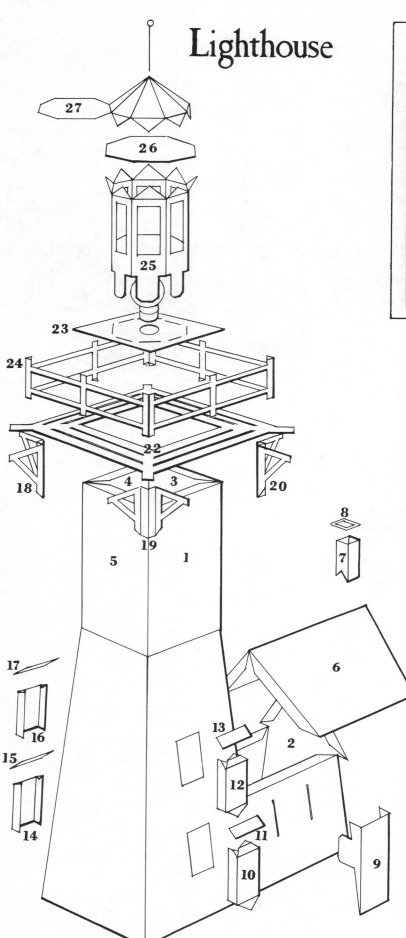

Instructions

The above photographs of the front and back views of the lighthouse and the exploded drawing to the left should greatly aid the reader in constructing the building. The following tools are recommended: an Exacto knife with a #11 blade, Elmers glue, a scoring tool for folds, a burnishing tool for applying pressure to glued joints difficult to reach with finger tips, and a straight edge ruler or plastic triangle for cutting and scoring.

Begin construction from the bottom and work toward the top, making sure the observation platform is positioned before roof of main tower is glued on. All glue tabs are indicated by dots. Do not use excess glue— it will seep out and mar the printed surface. After glueing allow tab to dry before further handling. X's indicate areas to be cut-out.

Be sure to score all folds before bending. This will ensure accurate fits.

Small door leading to observation platform (on side 4) may be opened by cutting top left and bottom sides and scoring right side then bend in. Cut vertical slits (side 1) to receive tab of doorway projection. Cut indicated slits on top of main tower roof (piece 23) to receive tabs of lantern section (piece 25).

For a touch of realism, a flashlight bulb (General Electric PR2) may be inserted thru hole in main tower roof (piece 23). Be sure to insert bulb before positioning lantern section (piece 25).

When lantern roof is put on, completing the structure, a lightning rod may be created by inserting a ball headed 1″ pin thru point of roof top.

Mariners Church

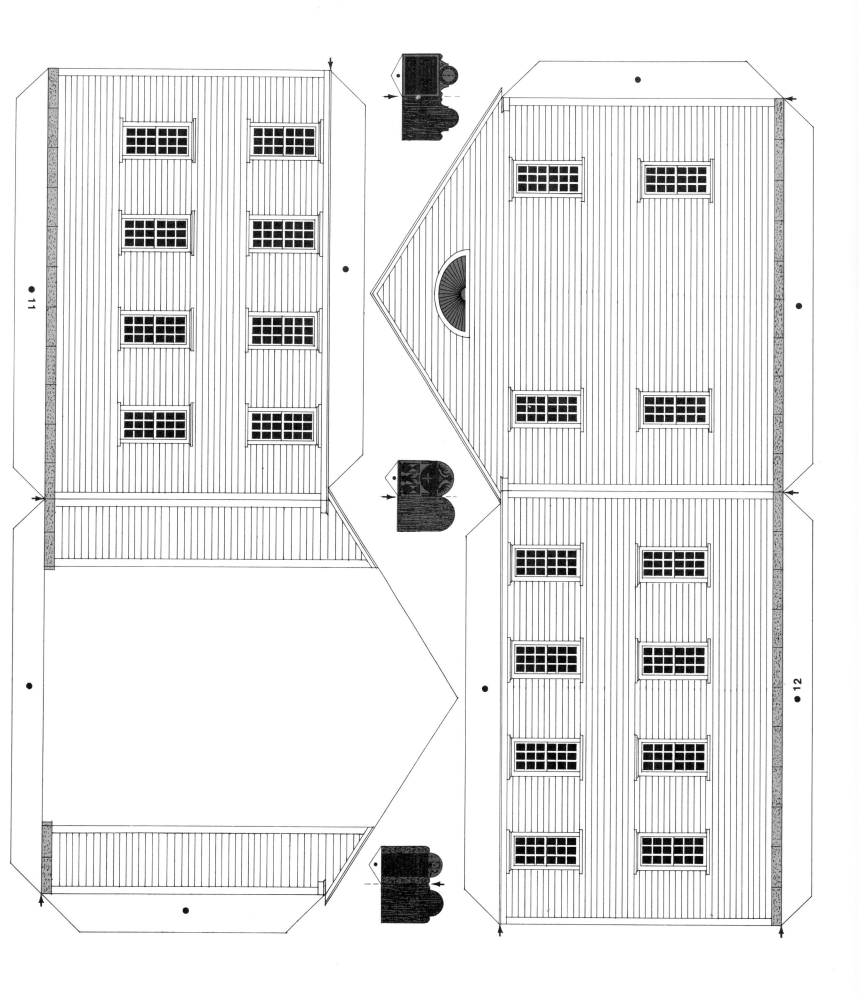

SCORE
RS REVERSE SCORE
CUT
X AREA TO BE CUT OUT

13

14

5

6

4

15

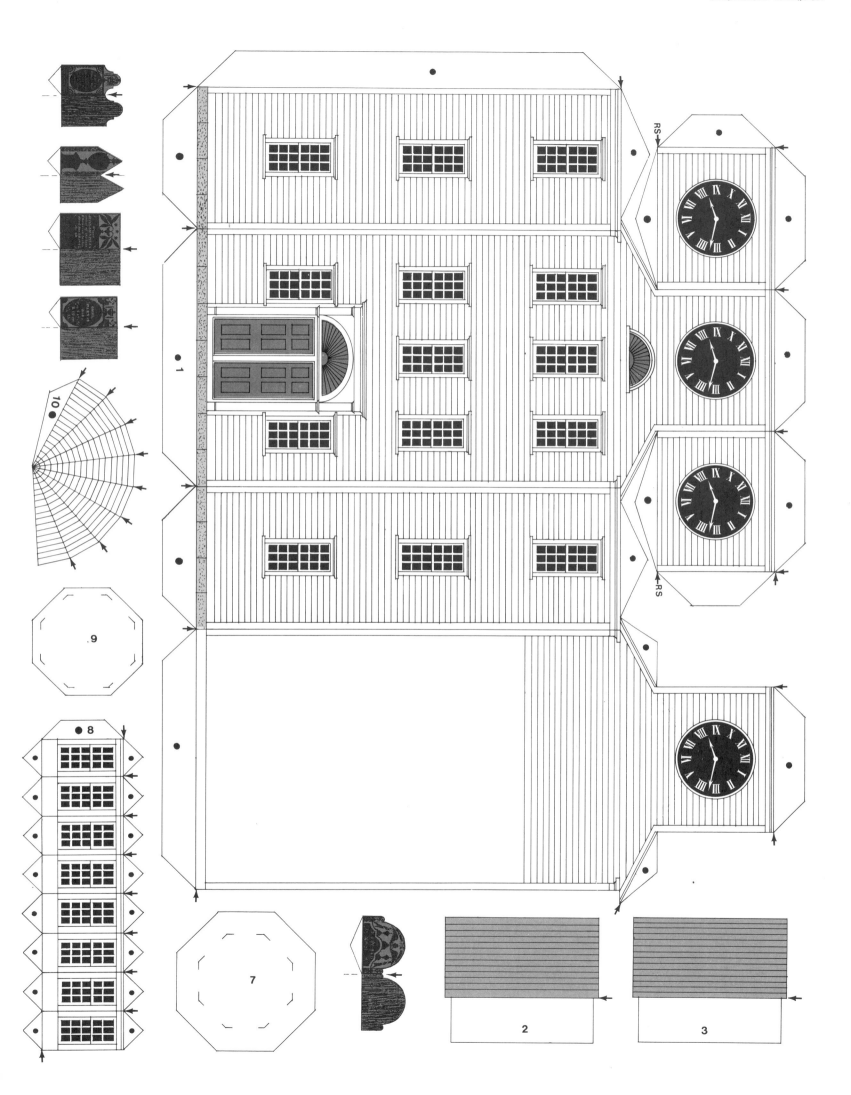

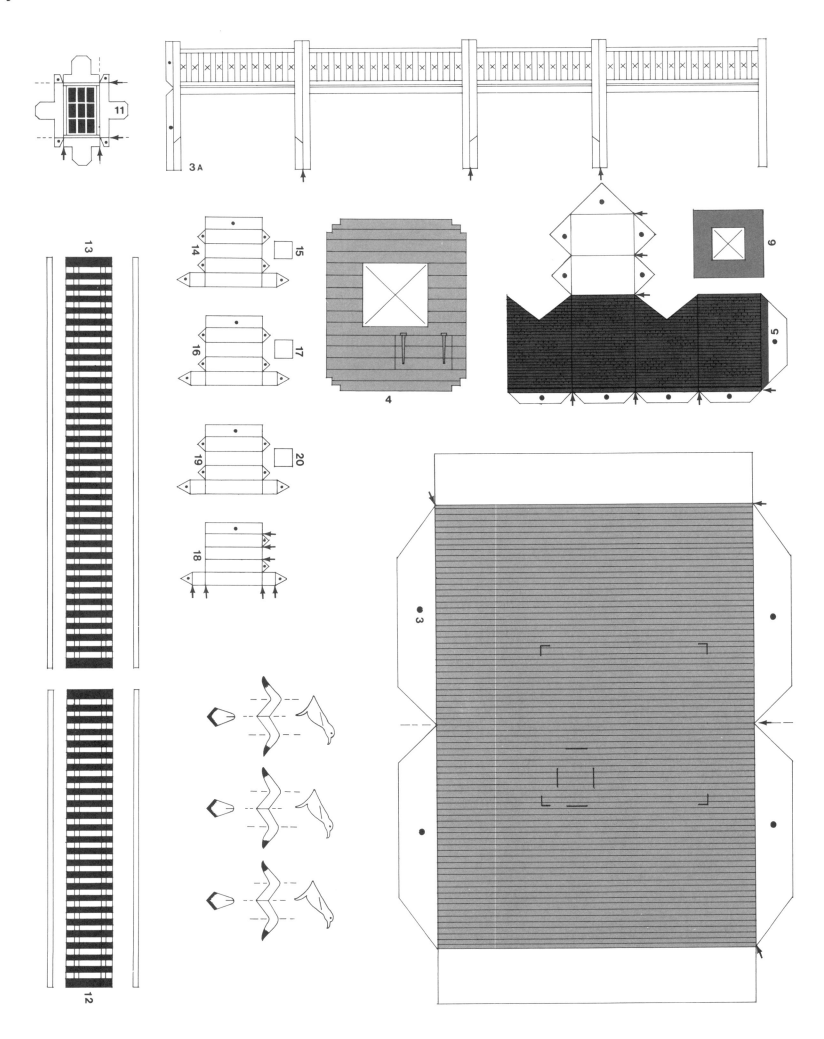

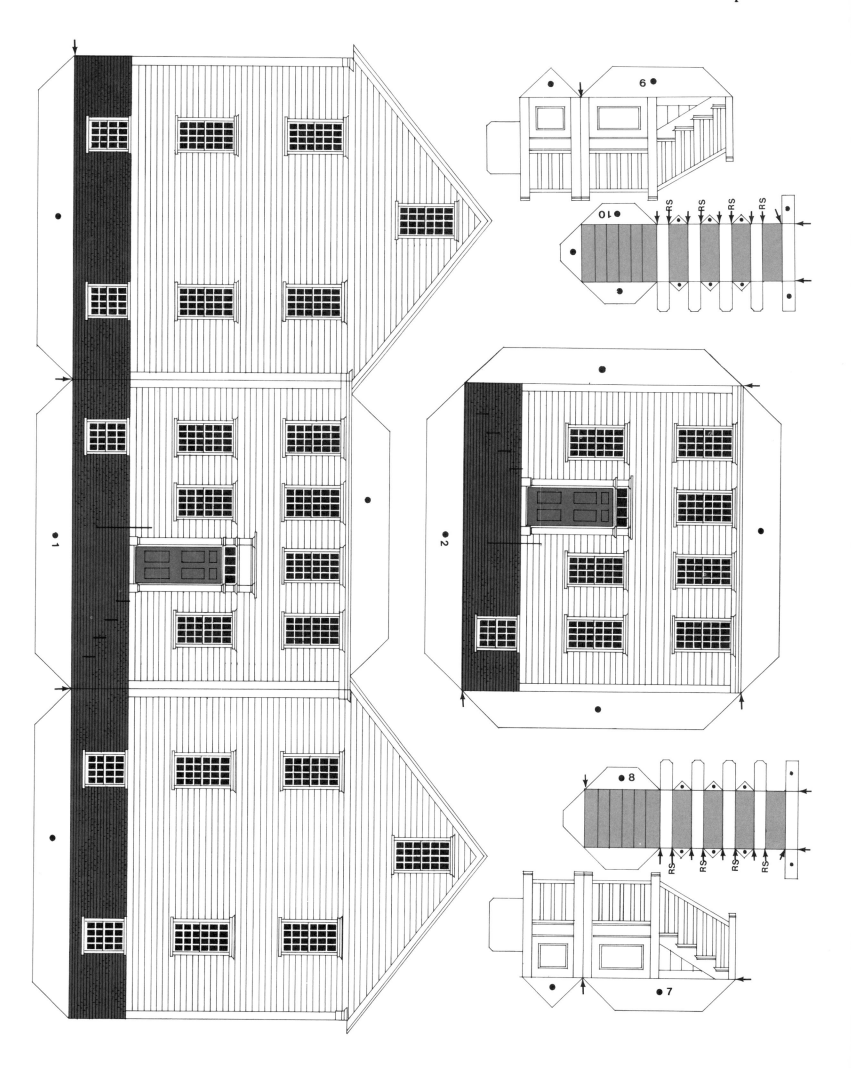

Lighthouse

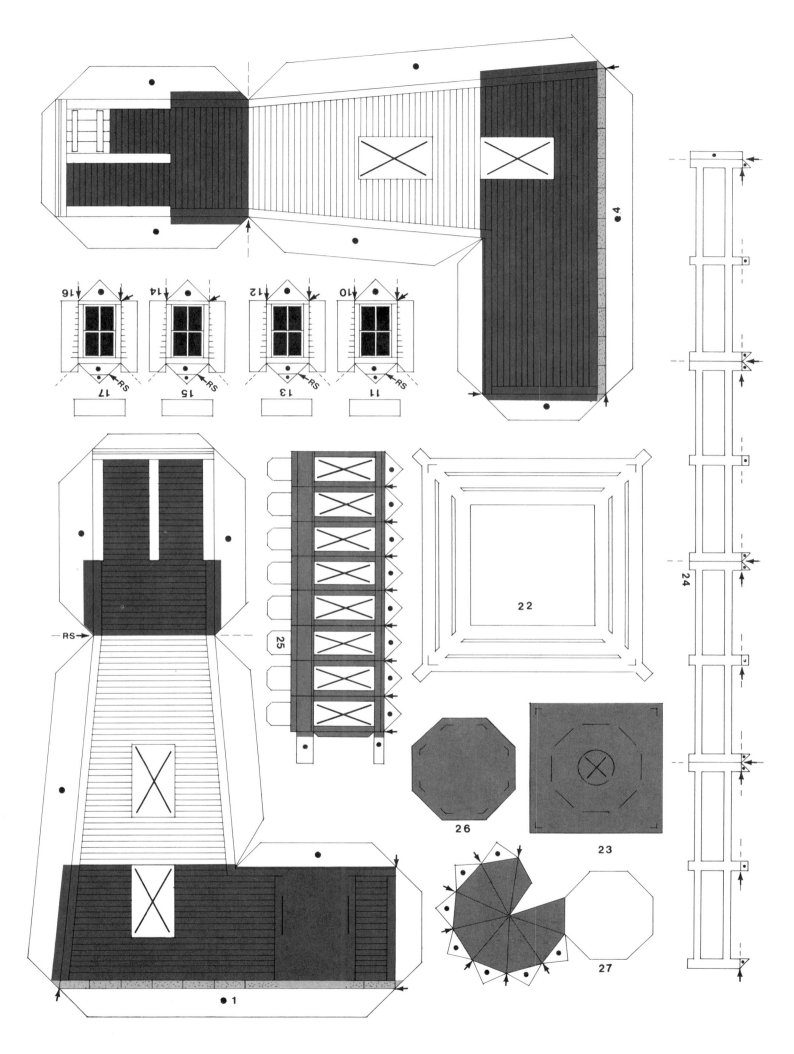

Custom House

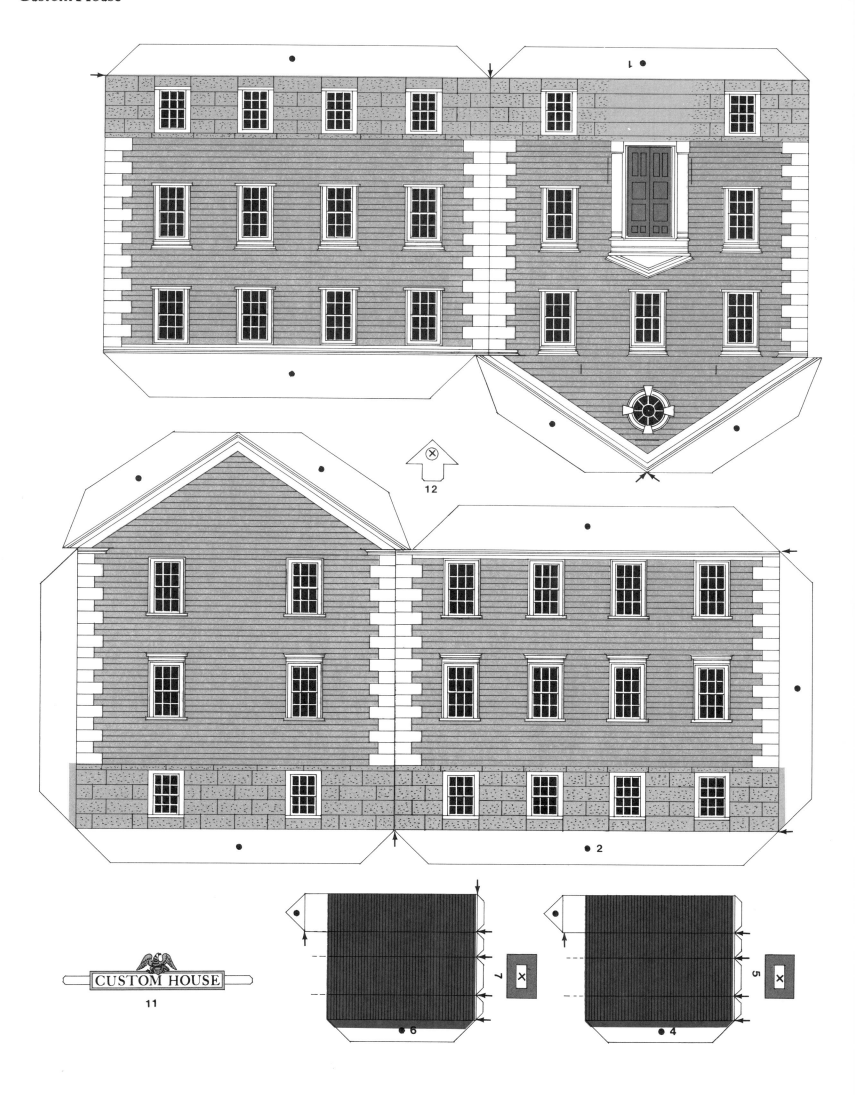

CUSTOM HOUSE

11

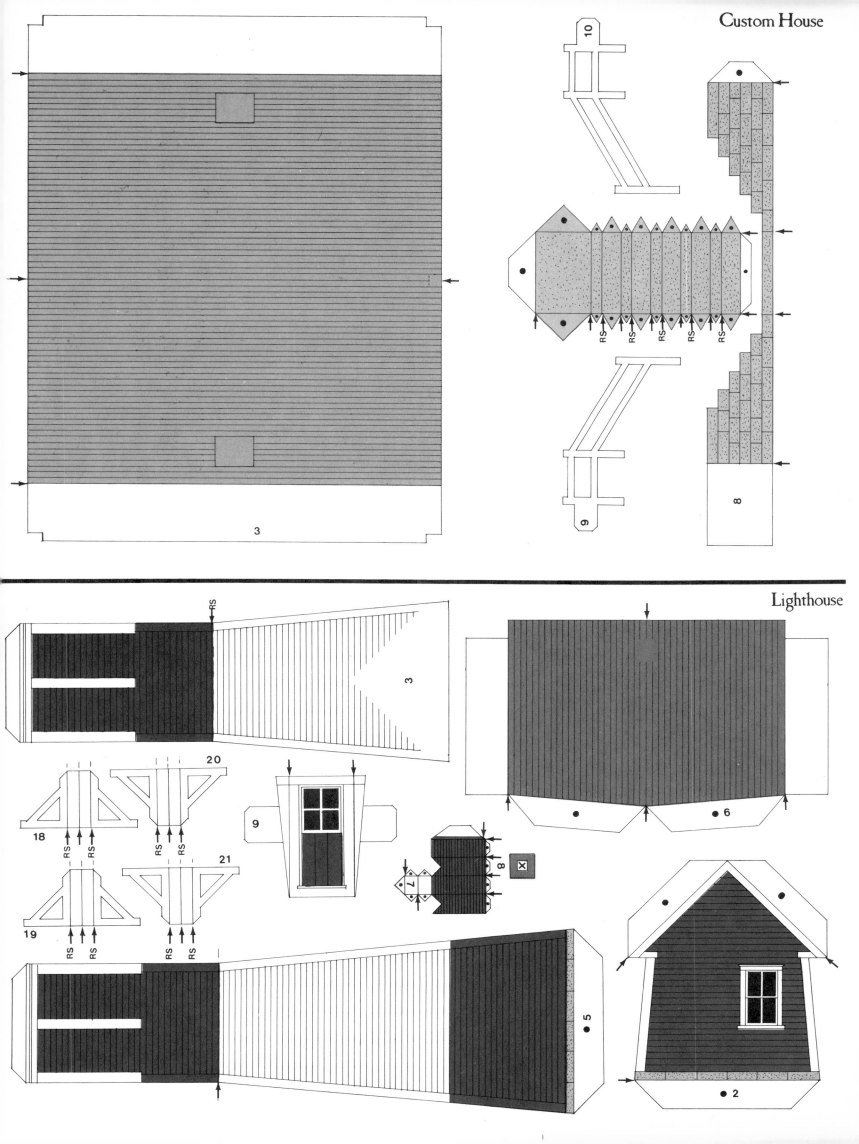

Custom House

Lighthouse

Gambrel Roofed Cottage

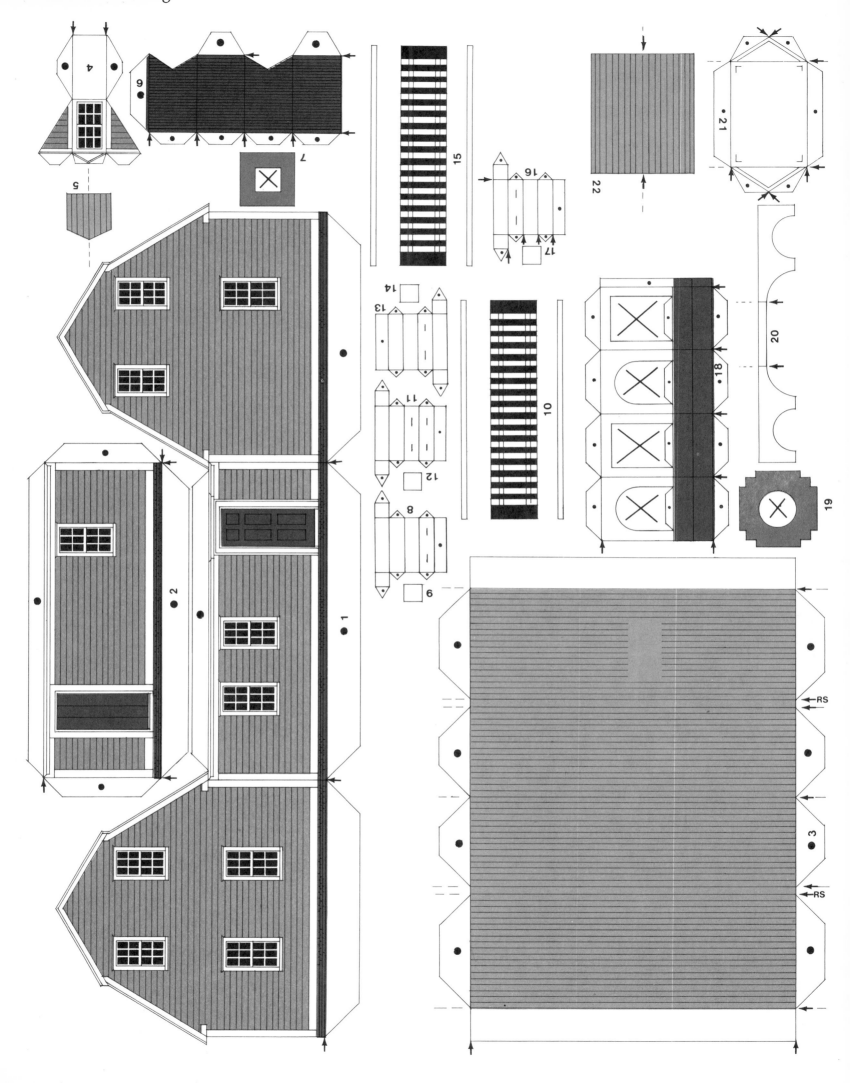

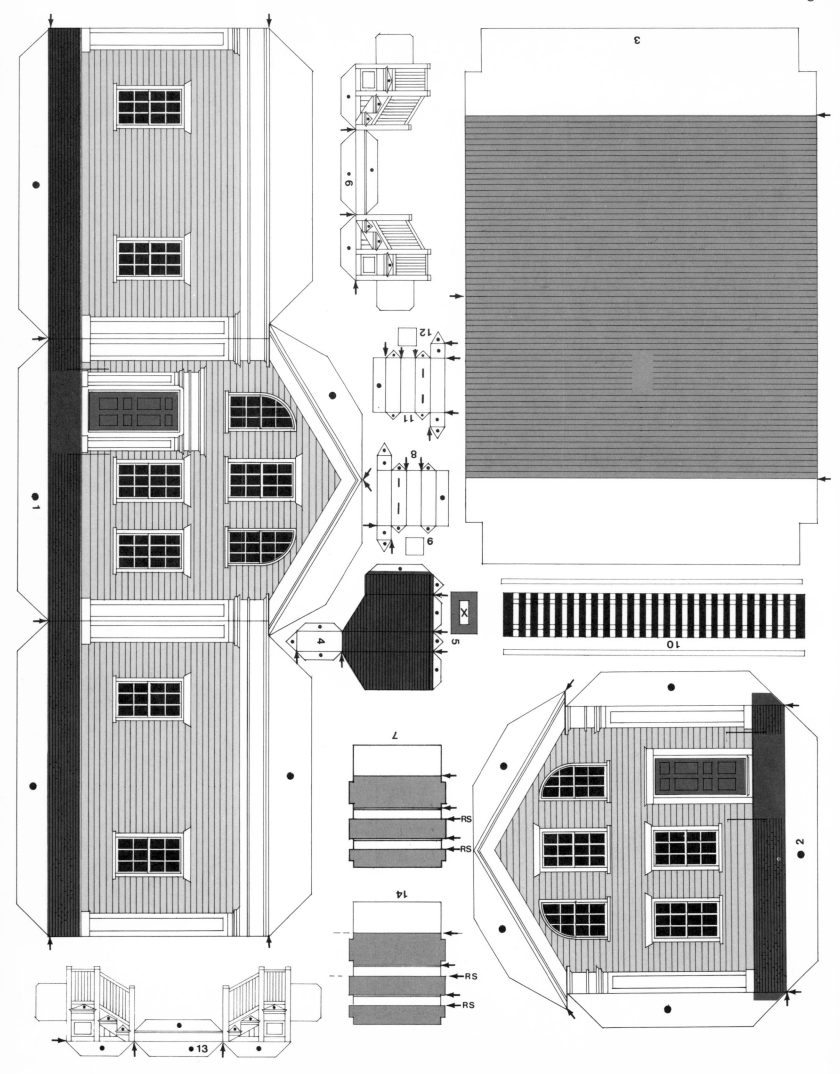

J. POTTLE, SHIPS CHANDLERY

29

J. POTTLE, SHIPS CHANDLERY

14

15

19

3

2

1

8

10